Juan Gris

© Ediciones Polígrafa, S. A.
Balmes, 54 – E-08007 Barcelona
www.edicionespoligrafa.com

Text by Rafael Jackson Martín
Translated by Sue Brownbridge

I.S.B.N.: 84-343-1079-1
Dep. legal: B. 19.415 - 2005 (Printed in Spain)
Printed by Mateu y Cromo (Madrid)

Juan Gris

Ediciones Polígrafa

Head of a Man – Self-portrait, *1916*

ARCHITECTURE AND COLOR:
THE PAINTINGS OF JUAN GRIS

Juan Gris has long been seen as the third member of a prodigious trinity that produced the very best Cubist painting. First came Picasso and Braque and then —following in their footsteps—came the modest, disciplined Gris. In addition to this view of Gris as one of the three key artists of the movement, the painter also came to be seen as a kind of apostle of Cubism, always ready to win over new converts or to take on those who did not believe in his faith. "The poor Gris, who explained Cubism, is mad," the sculptor Manolo Hugué remarked on Gris' convoluted arguments. Though these views of the painter do indeed contain an element of truth, Juan Gris should nevertheless be seen as an artist in his own right, not as an artist overshadowed by Picasso and certainly not the artist portrayed in the exaggerated and hence misguided remark of Manolo Hugué.

Juan Gris' pencil reproduction of one of Cézanne's best known pieces, The Bathers, *a key work in the art prior to Cubism.*

SCIENTIFIC CUBISM

To understand Juan Gris' important place in the history of art, we must closely analyze his concept of Cubism, which was entirely in keeping with his notion of painting as a whole. Gris strove unceasingly to remain faithful to his personal expression of the language of Cubism. Despite his initial admiration for the analytical Cubism of Pablo Picasso and Georges Braque, his early links with the Puteaux group—formed by Marcel Duchamp and his brothers Jacques Villon and Raymond Duchamp-Villon (all three of whom were fascinated by mathematics), as well as Albert Gleizes, Jean Metzinger and Louis Marcoussis—led him towards a more scientific and controlled concept of Cubism that was very different to the intuitive practice of Braque and the capricious brilliance of Picasso. As a result, Gris arrived at the Cubism of "the set square and the t-square"—as the poet Gerardo Diego described it on a number of occasions—reinforced by his close reading of textbooks on geometry such as the classic by Henri Poincaré.

Camille Corot: Girl with a Mandolin, *1860–65. Gris wanted his works to be classical in structure and Cubist in language. With this aim in mind, he took this painting by Corot as a pretext for his experiments in form (p. 57).*

ARCHITECTURAL ASPECT

In contrast with Picasso's concept of Cubism, expressed in compositions that take reality as their starting point and then transform it in successive phases, Gris established what he termed an "art of synthesis or deductive art." As Gris himself remarked, "Cézanne made a cylinder out of a bottle. I start from the cylinder to create a special kind of object. I make a bottle, a particular type of bottle, out of a cylinder." In short, first comes the imaginary concept of the painting and then its confrontation with reality: archetypal structure and construction in keeping with the purest Synthetic Cubism. As Gris saw it, painting has an architectural aspect founded on mathematics, a science that he believed the painter should study rationally and which, in his view, should never lead the artist along the

Place Ravignan, 1912.
*One of the views near the painter's studio
in the area around the hill of Montmartre.*

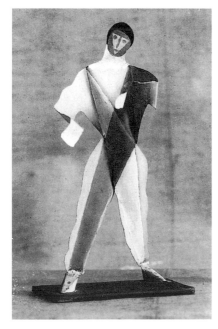

In 1923, Juan Gris produced this Pierrot,
*a small sculpture made of cut and painted
sheet metal that is evidently Cubist in tone.*

tortuous path of Abstraction. In short, painting should be humanized. In other words, it should be expressed through the space, color and the relations between the objects. "The only possible pictorial technique," Gris averred, "is a kind of flat, colored architecture."

THE RETURN TO ORDER

Even though Juan Gris was vehement in his assertions, his painting is not monolithic in character. One might describe his style during the war as contraband Cubism, as the critics of the movement accused it of being Germanophile. His complete devotion to Cubism took on the traits of a veritable declaration of faith as Picasso began gradually to abandon it, having trivialized it by turning it into just one of the devices in his wide-ranging repertoire when he tired of painting in the manner of the classics. Gris' Cubism at this time was, therefore, more sincere and bolder than that of Picasso, even though he still looked to his compatriot as his principal source of inspiration. This was also one of Gris' most productive periods, as this was the time when he began to experiment with a Cubism full of shadows and painted collages, and to invent the rhymes or repetitions of motifs with which he structured, in compositional terms, the entire pictorial surface. Even though Gris was a fervent admirer of the paintings he saw during his frequent visits to the Louvre, he remained unsure of the "return to order", a tendency that, after the war, rejected outright the radical experiments of the Avant-garde prior to the conflict and opted instead for an uncompromising return to figuration. When the Cubists began to parody classical painting in an attempt to legitimize themselves by establishing genealogical connections with tradition, Gris defined his method in similar terms. This led him to declare that his technique was "classical", because he had learned it "from the masters of the past." His rejection of Abstraction did not prevent him from spurning Naturalism, which reduces the painting to a mere copy of reality. But it was difficult to maintain a balance between the two elements, and even Gris was unable to achieve what he sought so hard to do. The prime movers of Cubism destroyed the traditional concept of the space but however much they formulated a new way of depicting or remaking the world, in the end they reduced their ambitious enterprise to residual vestiges or knowing winks that, as time passed, became devoid of meaning.

THE SILENCE OF THE CRAFTSMAN

Juan Gris was unquestionably a painter in the classical meaning of the term. He was interested in nothing but painting and lived solely for it. The Avant-garde was already moving in other directions, however, and his concept of the artist was at risk of disappearing amidst the tumult of the younger generations. The image of the artist as researcher, as expressed in Gris' pictorial work and in his insightful essays on theory, was swallowed up by the provocative action of the Dadaists and Surrealists. When they sent insulting letters to a number of Cubist painters and the movement's most eminent theorists, Gris took it as a personal insult in spite of his friendship with Surrealist painters and writers such as Masson, Artaud, Tual and Leiris. Gris countered the brilliant excesses of Picasso, that capricious sorcerer in the fascinating kingdom of art, with his silent humility of the craftsman working away, pursuing his research—always dissatisfied, always alert—and zealously employing the techniques that he was heir to in the private sanctuary of his studio.

JUAN GRIS, 1887–1927

Many artists are recorded in the history of art under a pseudonym. Juan Gris is one of them. Born in Madrid, a cultural backwater at that time, José Victoriano González, as Gris was named, soon learned to make the most of the few artistic opportunities that the Spanish capital afforded his busy mind. While he was studying with little enthusiasm at the School of Arts and Crafts, he blossomed artistically by producing drawings in the Modernist spirit published in popular periodicals of the time, such as *Blanco y Negro* and *Madrid Cómico*.

Juan Gris in a portrait by his friend Vázquez Díaz done in the autumn of 1906, when the two artists were sharing a studio.

PARIS AND CUBISM

Prompted perhaps by a wish to avoid having to do his military service, and aided by his friend the painter Daniel Vázquez Díaz, Gris left Madrid in 1906 to make his way to Paris, where he moved into his friend's studio. Not long afterwards, Vázquez Díaz introduced Gris to Picasso. Seduced by the artistic circles in which the artist from Malaga moved—which included painters such as Braque, poets such as Apollinaire and Max Jacob, and art dealers such as Daniel-Henry Kahnweiler—he took a studio next door to Picasso's in the Bateau-Lavoir, a building that stood at the foot of the hill of Montmartre, and began to earn a meager living as an illustrator. Though Gris' admission to the Avant-garde milieu of Paris did not translate into his automatic adoption of painting—his first oils date from 1911—the powerful influence of Braque and Picasso's Cubism and his contacts with the Cubist group in Puteaux quickly led him to embrace their pictorial language. The friendship between Gris and Picasso, whom Gris admired and to whom he paid an affectionate pictorial tribute in his first exhibition in 1912, eventually cooled, perhaps as a result of Gris' espousal of Cubism or because of some dispute of which we are unaware. Whatever the reasons, the

Amedeo Modigliani: Juan Gris, *c. 1915.*

Page published in L'Assiette au Beurre *in 1908. Another example of Gris' work as an illustrator that appeared in popular reviews of the period.*

Bookplate for the Editorial Pueyo in Madrid, one of the first known works by Gris before he moved to Paris.

comments in the book of memoirs by Fernande Olivier, Picasso's first companion, confirm the couple's suspicions of the Cubist neophyte: "Juan Gris, who had no great gifts but was shrewd, immediately followed the Cubist movement. He studied what one might call the tricks of Cubism and used them with a certain intelligence but no art."

THE *PAPIERS COLLÉS*

The brief but dazzling appearance of the *papiers collés*—pieces of paper stuck onto works—in Gris' artistic output in 1913 coincided with his adoption of Synthetic Cubism and with his holidays in Céret, where he produced landscapes in a range of colors very different to those of the Cubist palette. This was also the year when he defended his artistic theories in the face of opposition from other artists, among them the sculptor Manolo Hugué. That selfsame year, Gertrude Stein, the American writer and collector who had moved to Paris at the start of the century, bought her first paintings by Gris, at the same time extending her friendship and economic support to the painter in his times of greatest need. The depth of this friendship was to be demonstrated in each and every one of her future writings on the artist from Madrid.

COLLIOURE AND THE WAR

In the early years of the First World War, Gris was in a state of tormented anxiety touching both his personal life and his art. Shortly after the war broke out, he and his wife, Josette, fled from Paris to the fishing village of Collioure. There they lived for few months, constantly harassed by the police because of the artist's status as a foreigner. His sole fond memory of that time was his friendship with Matisse, whom he evokes in the compositions of windows that he was soon to begin painting. His work from that time is somber and disturbed and hence a faithful reflection of his life. "I sometimes feel that my way of painting is completely wrong," Gris wrote in a letter to his friend, the art dealer Kahnweiler. "I can find no place in my paintings for that sensitive and sensual side that should, it seems to me, always be present." Even though Gris produced his most significant pieces during this period, it was also a time when he pondered on the meaning of Cubism, observing that his former comrades were the first to abandon Cubism: Picasso was working on bucolic compositions close to Classicism, whereas Braque returned from the war front, recovered from his wounds and then adopted a course that seemed unlike his Cubist period. Juan Gris' last ten years of life were the bubbling 1920s. In 1920, Gris was diagnosed with a severe lung disorder. Despite occasional periods of respite, his weak lungs eventually led to his death. In 1921, he received his first commission from the director of the Ballets Russes, Sergey Diaghilev, to produce the set for the *Cuadro Flamenco*. Just as Gris accepted the commission, he learned that Picasso had maliciously taken over the project. Despite this setback, Gris went on to design various sets for Diaghilev's company in 1923, but his constant disgust at the poor transposition of his sketches to the final sets and at the frivolous climate surrounding Diaghilev and his artistic and literary coterie on the Riviera eventually put a halt to such collaborative ventures with the ballet company.

A BITTER-SWEET END

The warm and cheerful atmosphere of the Mediterranean inspired Gris, despite all the difficulties he faced, to produce a remarkable series of still lifes with windows, in which he reveals an amiable streak at a time when he was also painting compositions of melancholic subjects. In his still lifes, the emphatic forms of Cubism are muted to the point that they seem to anticipate the soft forms of Dalí, but in the other pieces he deliberately abandons Cubism, taking a more naturalistic approach that is more serene in spirit and more in keeping with the tastes of the "return to order". And so he developed his style of the closing years of his life, which was almost monastic in regime, with painting in the mornings and rest and drawing in the afternoons, until a complication of his lung disorder finally ended his life in 1927. Sadly, Juan Gris' death went largely unreported, nor did it lead to an immediate reappraisal of his work. It was several years before he became widely recognized as one of the great masters of Cubism.

Portrait of Daniel-Henry Kahnweiler, 1921.
Gris uses a few graphic lines to portray the German art dealer who supported Cubism.

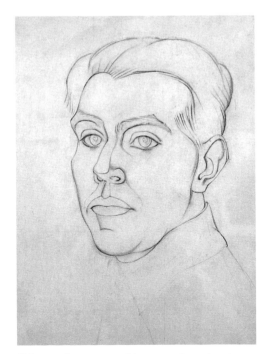

Gris uses the same graphic approach employed in his portrait of Kahnweiler to produce a portrait of himself, shown here at the age of 34.

INITIATION INTO CUBISM

Juan Gris' early paintings are characterized by his gradual adoption of the Cubist idiom. Starting from formal premises indebted to Cézanne, Gris arrived at Analytical Cubism in the brief space of two years. Nevertheless, there are more differences than similarities between his work and the Cubism of Picasso and Braque. He found it difficult to restrict his palette to the ochers, earthy colors and grays characteristic of the other two artists, as a result of which his compositions often look brighter. Moreover, forms in Gris' works are broken down into fewer facets and hence are less explosive, as if they were resisting the lure of Abstraction. Lastly, the motifs in these works are in most cases easily recognizable and so he has no need of the characteristic signs employed by Picasso and Braque which, in the manner of hieroglyphics, help the viewer to identify the motif depicted.

Siphon and Bottles, *1910.* Three Oil Lamps, *1910-1911.* Bottle and Pitcher, *1911.*
The simplicity of the composition is in keeping with the austerity of the still lifes by Cézanne. Even though the objects are perfectly recognizable, the rigidity of the Cubist framework that envelops and hardens them, the restricted range of colors and the short, parallel, vibrant brushstrokes reveal the close links between these and the early experiments in Analytical Cubism.

Portrait of M. Legna, *1911. This work is indebted to the heads painted and sculpted by Picasso in 1909, and is noteworthy for the blending of different viewpoints into a single two-dimensional image. The face is transformed into a synthesis of the views from the front and in profile, which is characterized by the eye and the line bisecting the chin.*

Portrait of Picasso, *1912. This portrait is first and foremost a public expression of the pupil's recognition of his master, here portrayed in the traditional manner, palette in hand. The most notable features of the painting are the restriction of the colors to the analytical grisaille, the rejection of chiaroscuro and the use of a single source of light. Two portraits by Picasso serve as points of reference for this tribute to him: the first of them, his portrait of Gertrude Stein, as revealed in the pose of the subject; and the second, his painting of Ambroise Vollard, as demonstrated by the treatment of the pictorial surface.*

Bottles and Knife, *1912. This piece represents another step in the gradual subjection of the still life to the Cubist structure. In this case, the diagonal lines transform the pictorial image into a kaleidoscopic view. The lack of any surrounding space makes the objects seem suspended. Nevertheless, there is an evident discrepancy between the unreal treatment of the space and the "realistic" study of the light, which illuminates the entire composition from the top left vertex of the painting.*

Glass and Bottles, *1912. In his experiments related to the findings of Picasso and Braque around 1910-1911, Gris opted for a more orthodox composition delimited by a grid of horizontal and vertical axes, and chose to completely shun naturalism.*

Man in the Café, *1912. The caricaturesque air of the subject and the emphatic figurative accent of the painting call to mind Gris' beginnings as a satirical illustrator. Nevertheless, the abrupt merging of the interior of the café and the exterior, represented by the awning and the buildings in the background, seem to herald his still lifes and subjects posing in front of windows.*

Still Life with Guitar, *1912–1913*. Guitar and Glass, *1912. One of the notable features of Gris'*
painting from 1912 is his extensive use of black, white and gray, whereas there is a an
explosion of colors in the dramatic polychromy of his works from 1913, in which the almost
linear brushstrokes found the year before have now matured. Following his doubts and
contradictions of 1912, Gris' enormous talent for coding and his compositional system are
revealed. Here he arrived at an impressive gravity of expression and rigor in execution.

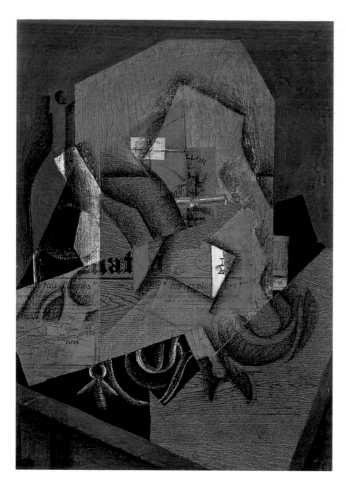

PAPIERS COLLÉS

Even though Gris had already experimented with the possibilities of collage by including bits of mirror or labels in his paintings, it was not until 1914 that he began to devote himself almost exclusively to the use of *papiers collés*. Broadly speaking, Gris' works retain the hallmarks of the Cubist collage: the rejection of imitated light and the concept of the painting as an object of value in itself—the *tableau objet*—and the denial of the painting's traditional representational function, the painting as a window onto a real or fictitious scene. Moreover, in his use of collage, Gris set out to contradict the true and the false, that which he had fashioned with his own hand and that which he had chosen to include in his pictorial composition. There are, however, significant differences between the *papiers collés* of Picasso and those of Gris. Picasso had no hesitation in imbuing his *papiers collés* with new values, for example by transforming a piece of wallpaper into a table cloth, whereas Gris preserved the original function of the objects he stuck to the pictorial surface.

The Packet of Coffee, *1914. Cubist painters did not include fragments of newspapers in their works for reasons solely to do with form but carefully selected the headlines and news that they stuck to their compositions as complementary thematic elements. This explains the choice of* ces explorateurs *(these explorers) by way of a tacit reference to the bold research of the Cubist painters.*

Bottle, *1914. This is a collage of rare beauty. The crystalline forms of the bottle are combined with the lightly drawn legs of a woman done in pencil, a disconcerting splitting in two that anticipates the anamorphoses of Surrealism.*

The Guitar, *1913. The use of* trompe l'œil *and the dominant vertical axes link this work with* Beer Glass and Cards *(p. 21). Gris incorporates a print in this work, a mechanically produced image that is in sharp contrast to the painted still life, but explains its inclusion by remarking "the print is not an essential component of the pictorial concept. Any new owner could change it for another element." Thus the painting is subject to a cycle of continuous change not wrought by the painter's hand.*

Guitar, Glass and a Bottle, *1914. This work is a strange combination of objects painted in a naturalistic manner and a disjointed guitar, which is shown from various viewpoints. The somber tone of the composition and the matching pairs of forms—note, for example, the repetition of the glasses—anticipate the large still lifes that he produced in the closing years of the second decade of the 20th century.*

Beer Glass and Cards, *1913. This painting is full of visual effects and* trompe l'œil *arranged in skillful dialectical contrast: the paper imitating the tiles is juxtaposed with the false marble of the table; the real cards appear next to the painted pipe. The composition is structured by vertical strips that offer a number of alternative viewpoints. The depiction of the beer glass, which is shown in elevation, in profile and as a cross section, is a prime example of "set square and t-square Cubism," the term that the poet Gerardo Diego used on more than one occasion to describe the style of his friend Juan Gris.*

Glasses and Newspapers, *1914. Glass and Packet of Tobacco, 1914. A number of different pictorial tendencies are to be found in these canvases. Though the omnipresent newspaper* Le Journal *and the packet of tobacco establish links with more orthodox Cubist still lifes, the simultaneous repetition of the glass throughout the first painting is without question in keeping with the pictorial approaches taken by Futurism as expressed in the works of Umberto Bocionni and Carlo Carrà.*

23

FLAT, COLORED ARCHITECTURE

Even though Juan Gris always believed that color was one of the weaknesses of his paintings, his chromatic treatment of his works, which is sometimes bright and always highly individual, resembles the pictorial concepts close to the Orphism of Robert Delaunay. The structure of Gris' works is founded on science, yet the same is not true of his use of color. It was not his intention to research the physics of color or the colors of the prism, nor was he concerned with the psychological and sensorial treatment of color by the Fauves. Even so, Gris understood full well that color is one of the principal generators of painting: "Cézanne moved towards architecture. I depart from it, hence I compose using abstractions (colors) and decide when these colors become objects." When color began to reappear in his works in the early 1920s—following a period in which shadows predominated—it transformed the architectural coldness of his structure into a warm, evocative lyricism full of poetry.

Guitar on a Table, 1915. Gris gave up his experiments with collage one year after enthusiastically adopting it in his works. In its place, he returned to painting based on visual illusions—in this case, the real effect of the painted wood—and on the distribution of the composition in superimposed planes lacking in tonal variety. The shallow depth of the work, which is only slightly intuited in the superimposition of the planes, and the pointillist surfaces of the background bear clear resemblances to the works being produced by Picasso at the same time.

Violin and Glass, *1913. This singular work is very different to the rest of Gris' oeuvre in format, as it is excessively oblong, and in the bright coloration, with its almost phosphorescent hues that are unlike the contemporary—and more orthodox—compositions of Braque and Picasso. This, together with the pronounced distortion of the objects, imbues this painting with a discouraging, supposedly Expressionist, air.*

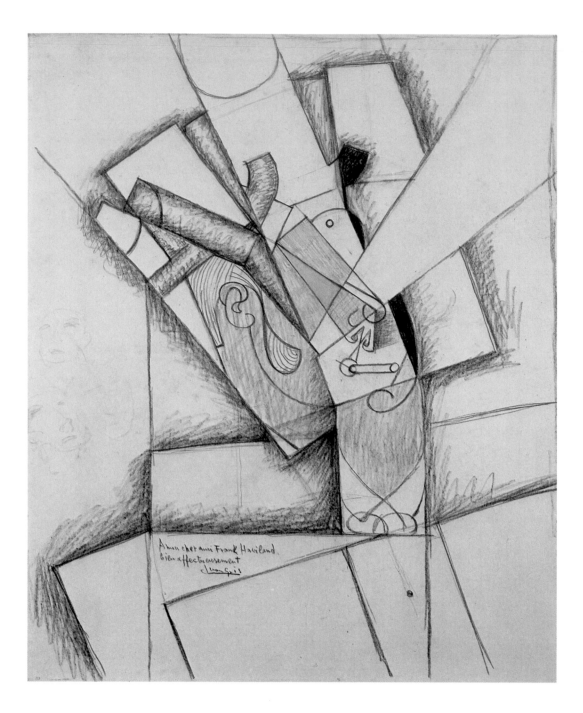

Study for "The Smoker", *1912*. The Smoker, *1913. A comparison of the drawing done of*
The Smoker in 1912 and the oil painting of the same title from 1913 reveals how the hatched
shadows in the earlier piece are transformed in the later work into black patches, which
makes the painting an almost flat, semi-abstract work, leaving aside the accidental vestiges
of a cartoon.

Saint-Matorel, *1913. This work, with its kaleidoscopic coloring, takes its title from a book by the poet Max Jacob, one of Juan Gris' friends from the time of the Bateau-Lavoir. The successful fusion of the different spatial planes, represented in the bottom half solely by chromatic devices, places this still life close to the luminously colored Abstraction of Robert Delaunay, who wrote various pieces on the subject, some of which Gris read.*

Landscape at Céret, *1913. Though the quality of this landscape cannot be compared with the still lifes Gris was doing at the time, it is nevertheless imbued with an originality unprecedented in the poetics of Cubism, which always showed little interest in the genre and would in any case never have conceived pictorially of nature in such succulent tones as these.*

Violin and Guitar, *1913*. Bottle and Glass, *1914*.
Despite his limited thematic repertoire,
Juan Gris' ability to surprise the spectator
is admirable, as is his capacity to capture
an object from different viewpoints without
stripping it of its structural harmony,
which remains largely unaltered by the
bold combination of warm and cold ranges
of colors.

Newspaper with Coffee Mill, *1915, and* The Breakfast, *1915. Gris showed a clear preference for still lifes to do with breakfast, hence cups and coffee mills are frequently found in his compositions of this type. These particular works even share the same formal concept, not just in their spatial organization and the dissection of the objects, but also in the distribution of the colors, with a single predominant color—blue in the first of these works and green in the second—in contrast with the visual illusions painted on several surfaces.*

Fruit Bowl with Bottle, *1916, and* Lamp, *1916. The essay by the Neo-Impressionist Paul Signac entitled* D'Eugène Delacroix au néo-impressionnisme *[From Eugène Delacroix to Neo-Impressionism], which deals with color in painting during the course of the 19th century, was republished in 1911. This, together with the use of vibrant pointillist surfaces in the Cubism of the early years of the war, brought the technique created by Georges Seurat into the modern era, though the Cubists employed it capriciously and not for the scientific purposes pursued by the French painter at the close of the 19th century.*

Violin before an Open Window, *1926. Gris met Henri Matisse in the fishing village of Collioure in 1915. Their friendship waned in the years after the war but slowly revived in the early 1920s. The flat distribution of the colors in this painting, made manifest in objects in a restrained manner by the graphic lines of their contours, indirectly evokes Matisse's techniques.*

The Singer, *1926. This portrait of a woman, imbued with a profound melancholy, combines the serenity of facial features that resemble those of Greek art—in vogue since the "return to order"—with the gross enlargement of the extremities, an approach employed by Picasso in his classical works. At the same time, the spatial box surrounding the figure and the window and railing in the background call to mind other more disturbing pieces by the painter from Malaga, first and foremost among them the enigmatic and irrational* Three Dancers *from 1925.*

PAINTING SHADOWS

Gris enveloped his compositions in darkness and shadows and hence rejected the use of bright colors. Nevertheless, it was not his intention to imbue his Cubist works from the time of the First World War with an irrational or tenebrist spirit, as he used the color black and its formal associations in a positive manner. His marvelous still lifes, in which he combines the object and its shadow, presence and absence, the empty and the full, advanced the initial formulations of Cubism and were connected to the new aesthetic of contemporary art. The void and shadows were now no longer associated with negative concepts—the lack of volume in the case of the void and the absence of light in the case of shadows— but were instead transformed into elements that built up the pictorial surface. Gris imbued this approach with new meaning in the human subjects in his works from the closing years of the second decade of the 20th century and in the 1920s, when shadow took on the Surreal, if not to say schizoid, nature of the double. With it he expressed the contradictions—the positive and the negative, sanity and dementia—that every human being carries within himself.

Fantomas (Pipe and Newspaper), *1915.*
Gris not only diligently studied treatises and books on the sciences but was also a great lover of popular literary works such as those by Alexandre Dumas or Fantômas, whose face looks out at us defiantly from the disjointed cover of the book. Gris is to be admired for his restraint in the trompe l'œil of the molding and the wood grain of the table, while lightly sketching in the still life using a few energetic lines already dominated by a few fragments in black.

The Violin, *1916. This is a sublime example of Gris' "flat, colored architecture". The color is superimposed arbitrarily on the architectural structure of the painting and on its lines of force, a device that Miró and Picasso were to make frequent use of later on.*

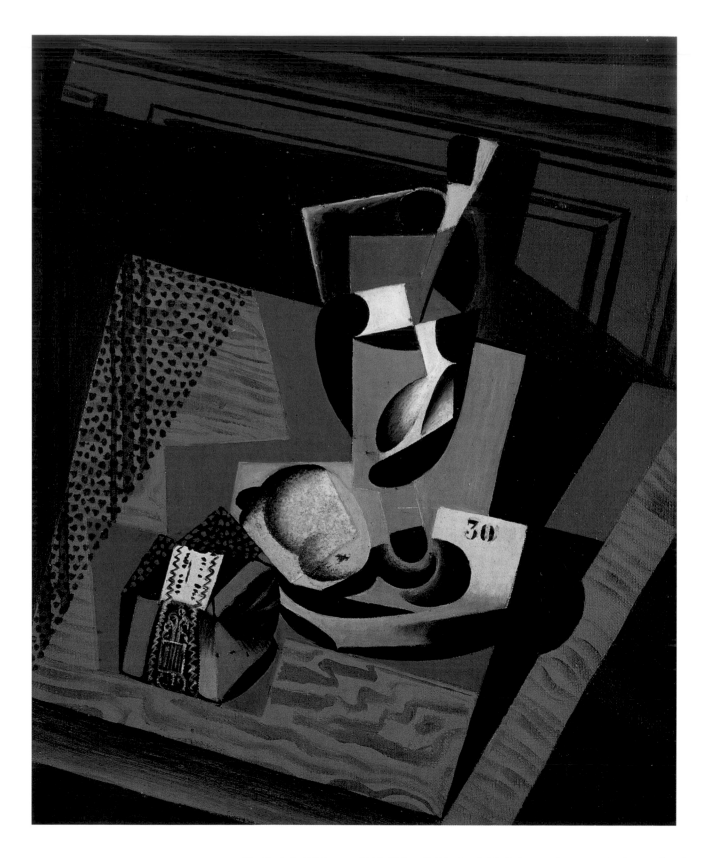

The Packet of Tobacco, *1916. This still life, in which Gris uses the same solutions as in other still lifes from the same year, is particularly noteworthy due to the naturalistic depiction of the lemon, the stenciled lettering—which rarely appears in his work, despite being common in Braque and Picasso's paintings—and the shadows around the glass, whose volutes imbue the object with a curious kind of baroque air.*

Fruit Dish, Glass and Lemon *(also known as* Still Life with Newspaper*), 1916. Similar in facture to* The Violin, *this painting is nevertheless even more somber in color. In it, Gris admirably combines the solid presence of the objects, concentrated in the succulent and naturalistic texture of the lemon, and their empty doubles, simultaneous visions of the objects and their silhouettes cut off against the background in half-darkness.*

Pitcher and Glass, *1916.* Fruit Dish and Glass,
1916. Still Life on a Table, *1916. It is worth
noting the asceticism of these three works
in which Gris combines the object and its
shadow, presence and absence, the empty and
the full, and in which black, ocher and white
predominate. In these compositions we find
all the qualities that Synthetic Cubism was
capable of. The various elements tend to come
together: as the objects become more refined
and lose their volume, so they communicate
a new sense of dynamism to the whole.*

The Strawberry Jam, *1917.* Still Life, *1917. In the year 1917, Gris suffered a number of bouts of severe depression in response not only to events in his personal life but also to his concept of painting. He understood that Cubism was a language in decline and that his solutions were likely to take him up a blind alley. Nevertheless, his mastery in handling whites and shadows —for example, the guitar that merges like a negative with the bottle—very closely resembles the future anamorphoses of the Surrealists.*

Harlequin with Guitar, *1919, and* Pierrot with Guitar, *1919. Cubist painters were not the first to portray characters from* Commedia dell'Arte, *but they were the ones to do so in the boldest, most symbolic manner. The solutions Gris arrived at delighted the Surrealists: the illuminated part of the faces and their shadows gave rise to a disturbing split in two that simultaneously represented the subject and his psyche.*

Pierrot, *1922. Even though this work resembles the previous two in the division of the subject's face, it is nevertheless different in two respects. In this painting, the face has been turned into a mask that calls to mind the solutions adopted in primitive art—it was at this time that Gris began to take an interest in tribal art—while the influence of his painter friend Fernand Léger is revealed in the pierrot's limbs, which imitate the texture of sheet metal that Léger was so fond of.*

 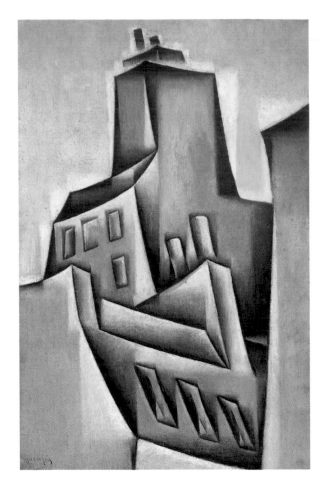

BUILDINGS

Landscape was not one of the Cubist painters' preferred genres. They restricted themselves to the portrayal of intimate everyday settings and sought to capture those elements that surrounded them in their studios, and so ignored the scenes of nature or urban images that filled the works of other Avant-garde movements such as Expressionism or Futurism. Juan Gris, however, did produce a number of such paintings, though he did not place the emphasis on either the wild or the sublime side of nature. Consequently, the human reference is a deliberate and fundamental element in these compositions by its very absence. The constructional character of Gris' Cubism, as well as his "architectural" concept of painting, is clearly reflected in the buildings and houses found in his few landscapes, and though such works may be limited in number, they are not without interest.

Houses in Paris – Place Ravignan, *1911.* Houses in Paris, *1911. These are two of Gris' earliest pictorial works and are already characterized by the austerity of the composition and the colors. The morphological distortion of the houses and the disturbing chiaroscuro give them a surprisingly Expressionist look: the buildings call to mind veins of quartz with angular edges and so can be seen as an anticipation of the Expressionist architecture of glass, a German tendency that sought around 1915 to replace brick with glass, thereby imbuing constructions with symbolism.*

Landscape with Houses in Céret, *1913. In this work, in which the landscape is depicted as a still life, Gris has preserved the diagonal lines of force that predominated in his still lifes of the year before. The composition of the painting is structured by two simultaneous viewpoints, one of them frontal and the other bird's eye. The range of colors Gris employs is even bolder than that of* Landscape at Céret *(p. 29), painted at the same time as this work.*

Houses at Beaulieu, *1918. Juan and Josette Gris spent the final months of the war in Beaulieu-
sur-Dordogne. It was here that Gris produced this landscape, in which the absence of any sense
of volume gives the work the look of a painted collage. The only note of warmth in this painting,
otherwise predominated by cold tones, like the sky in this region that Gris so loathed, is the
roof in a reddish and slate-like color that is typical of houses in this part of France.*

The Village, *1918. It is intriguing to note Gris' tendency to paint buildings along the lines
of supposedly Expressionist parameters. In this case, the angular houses and their set-like
distribution suggest the atmosphere of German films.* The Cabinet of Dr. Caligari, *made just
one year later, is instantly called to mind as one looks at this painting.*

INDOORS AND OUT

Gris painted still lifes in front of windows during two different periods of his career. In the first of these groups of works, produced during the First World War, the windows cast a cold, almost nocturnal, light on the objects in front of them. Later, under the kindly influence of the Mediterranean, he returns to the genre with a more optimistic range of colors. Many have tried to see a link between these works and those by Matisse, despite the formal differences between them, and in fact Gris' paintings more closely resemble pieces by Picasso. Another interesting aspect of this iconography lies in the function of the opening as a "painting within a painting", which harks back to the traditional notion of painting as a window. The idea of the Cubist painting as an object is thus tacitly rejected and the return to painting as a representational art is advocated.

Before the Window, *1921. Despite the use in this work of the devices typical of Cubism during the war, here we see a clear intention to accentuate the volumes rather than the planes characteristic of Cubist works of this time. The forms are almost perfectly delimited, and the solidity of the objects, as well as the almost metaphysical building in the background, draw links between this still life and the experiments in figuration of "the return to order."*

Still Life Before an Open Window: Place Ravignan, *1915. This is one of Juan Gris' best known works and is remarkable for the complex dialectical relationships established between the various elements. The still life is surrounded by the menacing darkness of night dissipated only slightly by the artificial light. The naturalistic and Cubist form of the objects, the crystalline facets distorting the letters of* Le Journal *and the alienated interpenetration of the indoor and outdoor spaces inject a sense of unease into a theme that the Cubists had depicted with objective intentions.*

Guitar and Fruit Dish, *1921. This painting, produced in Céret, where Gris and his wife had moved to due to his poor state of health, clearly reveals the differences between the still lifes with windows by Matisse and those painted by Gris. Whereas Matisse clearly distinguishes the indoor area from the exterior space, Gris extends beyond the window—as can be seen in this work— with the result that the bluish atmosphere penetrates and bathes the entire still life.*

Bananas, *1926. The soft forms and the graphic composition are the main characteristics of this syncopated still life, defined by its admirable serenity. Gris' profound depression in the months prior to his death is reflected in the lack of any vibrant color in his still lifes from 1921. In this particular work, moreover, the window is reduced to a dull blue rectangle.*

EVOCATION OF THE PAST

Juan Gris did not content himself with effecting a profound transformation in painting, as he aspired to do more. It was his wish to arrive at the materialization of a classical art expressed in a modern language: "I would like," he declared, "to continue the tradition of painting using artistic devices but to give it a new aesthetic based on the intellect. I believe it is possible to espouse Chardin's methods without adopting the appearance of his paintings or embracing his concept of reality." Gris went often to the Louvre and apart from a few exceptions, his references to the past, in particular from 1916 onwards, are not parodies or quotations from a specific painting. Above all else, Gris wanted his works to be classical in structure and Cubist in language. Of all the schools of the past, he preferred the French tradition—the oft mentioned influence of the Spanish Baroque is less clear—and it was in this that Gris strove to be included.

Still Life with Book, *1911.* Head of Harlequin (after Cézanne), *1916. 1906 was the year that Gris arrived in Paris and the year that Paul Cézanne died. The retrospective of Cézanne's work held just months after his death revealed his fascinating findings to an entire generation of artists. In this still life—one of Gris' very first—he already aspires to follow Cézanne's lead, as shown by the synthesis between a modern form and a serene composition, which harks back to the pure tradition of still lifes.*

Woman with a Mandolin (after Corot), *1916. The "return to order" encouraged artists to look to painters from the past, especially French painters such as Ingres, Cézanne and Corot. In this work by Gris, Corot's theme has been stripped of its lyricism and, now pervaded by objectivity, has become a mere pretext for experiments in form. Though the drawing makes reference to Corot's original (p. 5), the chromatic treatment of the surfaces is in keeping with Gris' Cubist style. Picasso was to conduct a similar experiment one year after Gris in* The Italian Girl, *another version of a theme by Corot.*

Still Life on Plaque, *1917. Employing a device first used by Picasso and Braque, Gris records his name and the date of this still life on the work as if they were chiseled into granite. In this way he ironically demonstrates a desire for his works to be hung in museums alongside European paintings from the past. The visual illusion of the granite texture is intriguing, as is the signature, which, though it seems to have been carved into the canvas, has in fact been painted on by the artist.*

View of the Bay, *1921. In 1921, Gris had the idea for a number of still lifes which he intended as an allegory on the senses, a popular theme among the Baroque painters. In this particular work, the objects are symbolic representations of the five senses: the musical score represents sight; the guitar, the sense of hearing; le pet, a scatological reference, the sense of smell; and the translucent sail, the sense of touch.*

The Musician's Table, *1926. Gris uses an artist's palette and musical instruments as attributes of the painter and the musician. This is an unusual device within the body of his work, though it was common in traditional still lifes, including those of Chardin, whom Gris admired, and in a number of contemporary pieces by Picasso.*

Woman with Basket, *1927. Gris' last pictorial work is a synthesis of his entire oeuvre, from the classical references to the glowing colors, from the Cubist collage to the total figuration. Next to the figure of Greek bearing is a mirror without the silvered glass, a disturbing frame in which Gris might be hinting at the nothingness waiting for him on the other side: the world of representation suddenly gives way to the world of shadows.*

LIST OF PLATES

p. 38
Fantomas (Pipe and Newspaper), *1915*.
Oil on canvas, 60 × 72 cm.
National Gallery of Art, Washington (Lester Dale Foundation).

p. 39
The Violin, *1916*.
Oil on three-ply panel, 116.5 × 73 cm.
Kunstmuseum, Basel.

p. 40
The Packet of Tobacco, *1916*.
Oil on canvas, 46 × 38 cm.
Private collection.

p. 41
Fruit Dish, Glass and Lemon (Still Life with Newspaper), *1916*.
Oil on canvas, 73 × 60 cm.
Phillips Collection, Washington.

p. 42
Pitcher and Glass, *1916*.
Oil on plywood, 46 × 38 cm.
Museo Nacional Centro de Arte Reina Sofía, Madrid.

p. 42
Fruit Dish and Glass *1916*.
Oil on plywood, 61 × 38 cm.
Galerie Louise Leiris, Paris.

p. 43
Still Life on a Table, *1916*.
Oil on plywood, 55 × 45.8 cm.
Private collection, Belp

p. 44
The Strawberry Jam, *1917*.
Oil on canvas.
Kunstmuseum, Basilea.

p. 45
Still Life, *1917*.
Oil on canvas, 73.5 × 91.5 cm.
The Minneapolis Institute of Art (John R. Van Derlip Foundation).

p. 46
Harlequin with Guitar, *1919*.
Oil on canvas, 116 × 89 cm.
Musée National d'Art Moderne, Centre de Création Industrielle, Paris. (Gift of Louise and Michel Leiris).

p. 46
Pierrot with Guitar, *1919*.
Oil on canvas, 90 × 73 cm.
Musée National d'Art Moderne, Centre de Création Industrielle, Paris.

p. 47
Pierrot, *1922*.
Oil on canvas, 100 × 65 cm.
Galerie Louise Leiris, Paris.

p. 48
Houses in Paris – Place Ravignan, *1911*.
Oil on canvas, 40 × 35 cm.
Sprengel Collection, Hanover.

p. 48
Houses in Paris, *1911*.
Oil on canvas, 52.4 × 34.3 cm.
The Solomon R. Guggenheim Museum of Art, New York.

p. 49
Landscape with Houses in Céret, *1913*.
Oil on canvas, 100 × 65 cm.
Private collection.

p. 50
Houses at Beaulieu, *1918*.
Oil on canvas, 90 × 64 cm.
Rijksmuseum Kröller-Müller, Otterlo.

p. 51
The Village, *1918*.
Oil on canvas, 55 × 74 cm.
Private collection.

p. 52
Before the Window, *1921*.
Oil on canvas, 61 × 95 cm.
Private collection.

p. 53
Still Life Before an Open Window: Place Ravignan, *1915*.
Oil on canvas, 116.5 × 89 cm.
Philadelphia Museum of Art (Louise and Walter Arensberg Collection).

p. 54
Guitar and Fruit Dish, *1921*.
Oil on canvas, 61 × 95 cm.
Private collection.

p. 55
Bananas, *1926*.
Oil on canvas, 73 × 60 cm.
Private collection.

p. 56
Still Life with Book, *1911*.
Oil on canvas, 55 × 46 cm.
Musée National d'Art Moderne, Centre de Création Industrielle, Paris (Gift of Louise and Michel Leiris).

p. 56
Head of Harlequin (after Cézanne), *1916*.
Pencil on paper, 25.5 × 20.5 cm.
Musée National d'Art Moderne, Centre de Création Industrielle, Paris.

p. 57
Woman with a Mandolin (after Corot), *1916*.
Oil on ply panel, 92 × 60 cm.
Kunstmuseum, Basel.

p. 58
Still Life on Plaque, *1917*.
Oil on canvas, 81 × 65.5 cm.
Kunstmuseum, Basel.

p. 59
View of the Bay, *1921*.
Oil on canvas, 65 × 100 cm.
Musée National d'Art Moderne, Centre de Création Industrielle, Paris (Gift of Louise and Michel Leiris).

p. 60
The Musician's Table, *1926*.
Oil on canvas, 81 × 100 cm.
Private collection.

p. 61
Woman with Basket, *1927*.
Oil on canvas, 92 × 73 cm.
Private collection.

SELECTED BIBLIOGRAPHY

Juan Gris. Peintures et dessins 1881-1927, *by Véronique Serrano and Nicolas Cendo. Musées de Marseille-Réunion des musées nationaux, 1998.*

DANIEL-HENRY KAHNWEILER. My Galleries and Painters. *Thames & Hudson, London, 1971.*

JUAN ANTONIO GAYA NUÑO. Juan Gris. *Ediciones Polígrafa, Barcelona, 1991.*

DANIEL-HENRY KAHNWEILER. Juan Gris. His Life and Work. *Thames & Hudson, London, 1969.*

CHRISTOPHER GREEN ET AL. Juan Gris. *Yale University Press, 1992.*